MOHAWK VALLEY LIBRARY ASSOCIATION
presents
SCIENCE
PHYSICS
GEOLOGY ECOLOGY
BIOLOGY ASTRONOMY
BOTANY CHEMISTRY
METEOROLOGY
ELECTRONICS
IN THE
SUMMER
DISCARD
sponsored by the
ELFUN Society:
A volunteer organization of General Electric Leaders
Hall of History Foundation

SCIENCE NEWS for KIDS

Food and Nutrition

Computers and Technology

Earth Science

The Environment

Food and Nutrition

Health and Medicine

Space and Astronomy

SCIENCE NEWS for KIDS

Food and Nutrition

Series Editor
Tara Koellhoffer

With a Foreword by
Emily Sohn,
Science News for Kids

Food and Nutrition

Chelsea Clubhouse
An imprint of Chelsea House Publishers
132 West 31st Street
New York NY 10001

For Library of Congress Cataloging-in-Publication Data, please contact the publisher.

ISBN 0-7910-9121-X

Text and cover design by Takeshi Takahashi
Layout by Ladybug Editorial & Design

Printed in the United States of America

Bang 10 9 8 7 6 5 4 3 2 1

This book is printed on acid-free paper.

Contents Overview

Detailed Table of Contents

by Emily Sohn
Science News for Kids

Science, for many kids, is just another subject in school. You may have biology tests and astronomy quizzes to study for, chemistry formulas to memorize, physics problems to work through, or current events to report on. All of it, after a while, can seem like a major drag.

Now, forget about all that, and think about your day. What did you eat for breakfast? How did you get to school and what did you think about along the way? What makes the room bright enough for you to see this book? How does the room stay cool or warm enough for you to be comfortable? What do you like to do for fun?

All of your answers, in some way, involve science. Food, transportation, electricity, toys, video games, animals, plants, your brain, the rest of your body: Behind the scenes of nearly anything you can think of, there are scientists trying to figure out how it works, how it came to be, or how to make it better. Science can explain why pizza and chocolate taste good. Science gives airplanes a lift. And science is behind the medicines that make your aches and pains go away. Most exciting of all, science never stands still.

Science News for Kids tracks the trends and delves into the discoveries that make life more interesting and more efficient every day. The stories in these volumes explore a tiny fraction of the grand scope of research happening around the world. These stories point out the questions that push scientists to probe ever deeper into physics, chemistry, biology, psychology, and more. Reading about the challenges of science will spark in you the same sort of curiosity that drives researchers to keep searching for answers, despite setbacks and failed experiments. The stories here may even inspire you to seek out your own solutions to the world's puzzles.

Being a scientist is hard work, but it can be one of the best jobs around. You may picture scientists always tinkering away in their labs, pouring chemicals into flasks and reading technical papers. Well, they do those things some of the time. But they also get to dig around in the dirt, blow things up, and even ride rockets into outer space. They travel around the world. They save lives. And, they get to spend most of their time thinking about the things that fascinate them most, all in the name of work.

Sometimes, researchers have revelations that change the way we think about the universe. Albert Einstein, for one, explained light, space, time, and other aspects of the physical world in radically new terms. He's perhaps the most famous scientist in history, thanks to his theories of relativity and other ideas. Likewise, James Watson and

Francis Crick forever changed the face of medicine when they first described the structure of the genetic material DNA in 1953. Today, doctors use information about DNA to explain why some people are likely to develop certain diseases and why others may have trouble reading or doing math. Police investigators rely on DNA to solve mysteries when they analyze hairs, blood, saliva, and remains at the scene of a crime. And scientists are now eagerly pursuing potential uses of DNA to cure cancer and other diseases.

Science can be about persistence and courage as much as it is about grand ideas. Society doesn't always welcome new ideas. Before Galileo Galilei became one of the first people to point a telescope at the sky in the early 1600s, for example, nearly everyone believed that the planets revolved around Earth. Galileo discovered four moons orbiting Jupiter. He saw that Venus has phases, like the moon. And he noticed spots on the sun and lumps on the moon's craggy face. All of these observations shook up the widely held view that the heavens were perfect, orderly, and centered on Earth. Galileo's ideas were so controversial, in fact, that he was forced to deny them to save his life. Even then, he was sentenced to imprisonment in his own home.

Since Galileo's time, the public has so completely accepted his views of the universe that space missions have been named after him, as have craters on the moon and on Mars. In 1969, Neil Armstrong became the first person to stand on the moon. Now, astronauts spend months in orbit, living on an international space station, floating in weightlessness. Spacecraft have landed on planets and moons as far away as Saturn. One probe recently slammed into a comet to collect information. With powerful telescopes, astronomers continue to spot undiscovered moons in our solar system, planets orbiting stars in other parts of our galaxy, and evidence of the strange behavior of black holes. New technologies continue to push the limits of what we can detect in outer space and what we know about how the universe formed.

Here on Earth, computer technology has transformed society in a short period of time. The first electronic digital computers, which appeared in the 1940s, took up entire rooms and weighed thousands of pounds. Decades passed before people started using their own PCs (personal computers) at home. Laptops came even later.

These days, it's hard to imagine life without computers. They track restaurant orders. They help stores process credit cards. They allow you to play video games, send e-mails and instant messages to your friends, and write reports that you can edit and print without ever picking up a pen. Doctors use computers to diagnose their patients, and banks use computers to keep track of our money. As computers become more and more popular, they continue to get smaller, more powerful, less expensive, and more integrated into our lives in ways we don't even notice.

Probes that fly to Pluto and computers the size of peas are major advances that don't happen overnight. Science is a process of small steps, and a new discovery often starts with a single question. Why, for example, do hurricanes and tsunamis form? What is it like at the center of Earth? Why do some types of french fries taste better than others? Research projects can also begin with observations. There are fewer tigers in India than there used to be, for instance. Kids now weigh more than they did a generation ago. Mars shows signs that the planet once supported life.

The next step is investigation, which can take on many forms, depending on the subject. Brain researchers, for one, often do experiments in their laboratories with the help of sophisticated equipment. In one type of neuroscience study, subjects repeatedly solve tasks while machines measure activity in their brains. Some environmental scientists who study climate, on the other hand, collect data by tracking weather patterns over the years. Paleontologists dig deep into the earth to look for clues about what the world was like when dinosaurs were alive. Anthropologists learn about other cultures by talking to people and collecting stories. Doctors monitor large numbers of patients taking a new drug or no drug to figure out whether a drug is safe and effective before others can use it.

Designing studies requires creativity, and scientists spend many years training to use the tools of their profession. Physicists need to learn complicated mathematical formulas. Ecologists make models that simulate interactions between species. Physicians learn the name of every bone and blood vessel in the body. The most basic tools, however, are ones that everyone has: our senses. The best way to start learning about the world through science is to pay attention to what you smell, taste, see, hear, and feel. Notice. Ask questions. Collect data. Do experiments. Draw tentative conclusions. Ask more questions.

Most importantly, leave no stone unturned. There's no limit to the topics available for research. Robots, computers, and new technologies in medicine are the waves of the future. Just as important, however, are studies of the past. Figuring out what Earth's climate used to be like and which animals and plants used to live here are the first steps toward understanding how the planet is changing and what those changes might mean for our future. And don't forget to look around at what's going on around you, right now. You might just be surprised at how many subjects you can find to investigate.

Ready to get started? The stories in this book are great sources of inspiration. Each of the articles comes directly from the *Science News for Kids* Website, which you can find online at *http://sciencenewsforkids.org*. All articles at the site, which is updated weekly, cover current events in science, and all are written with middle-school students in mind. If anything you read in this book sparks your interest, feel free to visit the Website to check out the latest developments and find out more.

And keep an eye out for an occasional feature called "News Detective." These essays describe what it's like to be a science journalist, roaming the world in search of scientists at work. Science writing is an often-overlooked career possibility, but science writers have endless opportunities to learn about many things at once, to share in the excitement of scientific discovery, and to help scientists get the word out about the significance of their work.

So, go ahead and turn the page. There's so much left to discover.

Section 1

Food for Health

Food is all around us. We use it to celebrate special occasions, to make ourselves feel better when we're sick or sad, and, of course, to stay alive. Because of the huge role food plays in our daily lives, it's no surprise that scientists have spent many years studying food and trying to determine which foods are best for our health.

Sometimes, it seems like a news report comes out every day telling us to avoid certain foods or to be sure to eat plenty of others. The advice we hear about food often seems to change as often as the weather! It's true that, over time, scientists discover new information about the nutritional value of foods and how they affect our bodies, and use those discoveries to make recommendations about what we should eat. As scientific knowledge about different foods grows, so does our understanding of the best things to eat to look and feel great.

One of the best sources for information about which foods to eat comes from the U.S. Department of Agriculture (USDA). It's called the Food Pyramid, and for many years, it has helped guide Americans of all ages in choosing a well-balanced diet. But the Food Pyramid has changed with the times. As food scientists learn more about nutrition and health, the USDA makes changes in the Food Pyramid to make use of the latest findings. The USDA issued the most recent Food Pyramid in early 2005.

The articles in this section examine the evolution of the Food Pyramid, and explores some of the other exciting new discoveries food scientists have made in recent years, including the role of "good" fats in maintaining our health and the dangers of being overweight.

—The Editor

Government Advice for Healthy Eating

Since the late 1800s, the United States Department of Agriculture (USDA) has been providing Americans with information about the nutritional value of different kinds of foods and advising citizens about which foods form the basis of a healthy diet. In the 1960s, medical professionals in the United States noticed an alarming increase in the incidence of heart disease and decided to create a system of guidelines to help people make better choices when planning their diets. In response, the government issued the first of its *Dietary Guidelines for Americans*, an information pamphlet that has been updated and reissued every five years. It was not until the 1980s, however, that the Food Pyramid was designed to serve as a graphic representation of the types of foods people should eat each day for a healthful lifestyle. In the following article, *Science News for Kids* writer Emily Sohn discusses the evolution of the Food Pyramid, highlighting its basic guidelines and examining the changes it has gone through over the years. Bear in mind that this article was written *before* the 2005 revised Food Pyramid was introduced.

—The Editor

ARTICLE

Building a Food Pyramid

by Emily Sohn

Before Reading:

- **Have you ever seen the Food Guide Pyramid? If so, where?**
- **What would you describe as a healthy, balanced meal?**

It's lunchtime, and you're hungry.

You have two choices. You can eat whole-grain rice, a big heap of steamed broccoli, and a grilled, skinless chicken breast. Or you can have french fries, a cheeseburger, and a chocolate milkshake. Which meal would you choose?

These are the kinds of decisions you'll have to make several times a day for the rest of your life. Carrot sticks or potato chips? Milk or soda? An apple or a candy bar?

Even when you know which choice is better for you, it still may be hard to resist foods that you find especially tasty. For many Americans, this means fried food, cookies, candy, and soft drinks.

All this sugar and fat, though, is starting to add up. Obesity is a growing problem in countries around the world. As waistlines expand, diabetes, heart disease, cancer, and other health problems are becoming more common—even among kids.

Scientists who study nutrition want to put an end to this alarming trend. Even governments are getting involved. They want to help people stay healthy and to keep health-care costs from spiraling higher.

For years, the United States government has recommended how much of different kinds of foods people should eat. You often see that advice displayed as a food pyramid. Foods near the bottom should be eaten much more often than those near the top.

Now that scientists have learned a lot more about which foods are good for you and which ones cause diseases, the government is updating its guidelines. There'll be new food advice by early 2005—and maybe you'll see a square, rectangle, or wheel instead of a pyramid!*

FOOD GUIDELINES

It's never too early to start eating well, says Mary Story. She's a nutritionist at the University of Minnesota in Minneapolis.

"What you eat now is certainly important for what you'll become," she says. "Eating healthy is also important for right now. It's tied directly to your energy level,

*Actually, the 2005 Food Pyramid has retained the traditional pyramid shape.

to the quality of your skin and hair, to feeling and looking good."

With these points in mind, the U.S. Department of Agriculture created the Food Guide Pyramid in 1992. Its shape was meant to illustrate the proportions of foods that should make up a healthy diet.

- **When was the Food Guide Pyramid created? Why?**

At the very top of the pyramid, where there isn't much room, are foods that shouldn't take up much room in your diet. Foods such as oil, butter, and sweets, for example, are best eaten in small quantities. Studies show that an overly fatty diet leads to heart disease and obesity.

One level down in the pyramid, where the triangle gets a little wider, are foods that are best eaten in moderation. The 2000 pyramid recommends two to three servings from the milk, cheese, and yogurt group. These foods contain calcium, which strengthens bones and prevents **osteoporosis**.

The Food Guide Pyramid also recommends two to three servings of protein, such as fish, beans, eggs, nuts, or chicken. **Protein** is important for your muscles, blood, immune system, and various processes in your body.

Another step down, the pyramid calls for three to five servings of vegetables and two to four servings of fruit. Fruits and vegetables are full of fiber, vitamins, and minerals that have been shown over and over again to prevent cancer, heart disease, and other ills.

At the bottom of the pyramid, where the triangle is widest, sit breads, cereal, rice, pasta, and other starches. You should eat 6 to 11 servings of these kinds of complex carbohydrates every day.

CHANGING THE PYRAMID

The pyramid's basic structure still makes sense to most nutritionists. Nonetheless, the U.S. Department of Agriculture has received plenty of criticism.

Story, for one, hopes the next pyramid will emphasize whole grains and high-fiber starches in the bread category. Studies have shown that whole-grain foods are much better for you than refined products and white bread.

- **What changes do some people want in the bread, cereal, rice, and pasta section of the pyramid?**

The pyramid categories also invite confusion. Does apple pie, for example, belong with sweets or fruits?

Another problem is portion size. There's a lot more supersizing of meals, for instance, than there used to be.

The next pyramid should be more specific about how big a serving is, Story says. Body size and activity level determine the number of calories people really need and the kinds of foods they should eat.

"A bagel at some of the bagel chains can be four servings of bread," Story says. "But people have no idea that bagels can be that dense." Eating foods in the right proportions doesn't help much if people are still eating too much.

PUBLIC COMMENTS

To come up with up-to-date food advice, a panel of 13 experts is now gathering information, arguing about evidence, and considering comments from the public.

People have offered all sorts of suggestions. A nutrition student from the University of the District of Columbia, for example, was one of many who wrote that the pyramid should encourage people to drink lots of water.

Other people thought the pyramid should distinguish between different kinds of fats. Saturated fats, found in butter, donuts, and many kinds of cookies, can lead to heart disease when eaten in large quantities.

Fats in nuts, seeds, and some fish, on the other hand, can help prevent disease. Eating nuts can actually help people stay slim, recent studies show. They keep you full longer, so you eat less.

- **What's the difference between the types of fats in nuts and fish and those often found in donuts or cookies?**

Some people, including vegetarians, choose to eat soy products, such as **tofu**, **tempeh**, and soy milk, instead of meat and dairy products. "Why is tofu not listed on the Food Guide Pyramid?" one person asked. "This is a complete protein, it's low in fat, and it has vital minerals, such as calcium and iron."

Another person suggested that the guidelines should warn against canned fruits and vegetables. These products often have large amounts of added sugar and salt.

Others wrote that exercise should earn a slot at the pyramid's base. Physical activity is good for the heart and muscles, it can boost moods, and it prevents obesity, among other health benefits.

The expert panel building the new Food Guide Pyramid has a tough job. The panel members have to choose among all these suggestions and come up with recommendations based on solid scientific evidence. The new food guide might not even fit comfortably into a pyramid.

STARTING EARLY

Of course, simply telling people what they should eat doesn't mean they'll do it.

In a study based on data collected in 1999 and 2000, the U.S. Department of Agriculture's Center for Nutrition Policy and Promotion found that only 10% of people had a healthy diet. The rest needed to improve their diets, especially by eating more fruit and dairy products.

Bad habits start early. Most surveys estimate that kids eat less than half the recommended amount of vegetables each day. Among the vegetables that kids and teenagers do eat, french fries make up a whopping 25%.

Just one child out of five eats five or more servings of fruit and vegetables each day, according to a recent study by scientists at Harvard University. And they found a curious trend: The more TV kids watch, the fewer fruits and vegetables they eat.

- **What have nutritionists found when it comes to kids and vegetables?**

So, try turning off the TV and start thinking about the Food Guide Pyramid next time you have to decide what to eat. Have an apple or orange after every meal. Drink milk or juice instead of soda. Eat whole wheat bread. Snack on carrot sticks rather than potato chips. Cut down on cookies and candy.

"You are what you eat," the old saying goes. When the new guidelines come out, scientists hope we'll all use them to live longer and healthier lives.

- **What are some snacks that this article recommends?**
- **Name three foods that are not mentioned in the pyramid but that some people think should be included.**

After Reading:

- What sorts of foods that are considered healthy do you enjoy eating?
- Why do you think there are so many overweight kids?
- Why do you think the U.S. government provides advice on what people should eat?
- Why do you think there seems to be a connection between watching TV and eating unhealthily? Based on your own observations, does this finding make sense? Why or why not?
- Why do you think people eat so many unhealthy foods? Do you think sugar and fried foods are addictive?

A New Food Pyramid

Since it was first created in the late 1980s and early 1990s, the USDA's Food Guide Pyramid has gone through many changes as medical professionals and food scientists have made discoveries about how different types of food affect the health and functioning of the human body. The most recent version of the Food Pyramid was issued in 2005. Although it still focuses on helping Americans choose the healthiest foods and avoid those that are high in fat and sugar, the new pyramid is different from those that came before it because it also emphasizes the importance of physical activity for good health. Writer Emily Sohn takes a look at the latest Food Guide Pyramid, showing how its new recommendations have stirred up some controversy.

—The Editor

Food for Life

by Emily Sohn

Before Reading:

- **Do you think that you eat healthily? Why or why not?**
- **Describe what you would consider a nutritious meal.**

A hamburger or a salad? A baked potato or french fries? A milkshake or orange juice? A candy bar or an apple? We have to make choices about what we eat every day.

New food guidelines and the food pyramid that goes with them emphasize that we should eat more fruits, more vegetables, and more whole grains than we typically do now. We should also avoid lots of sugar, salt, and certain types of fats. And we should get plenty of exercise.

As a young person, you might not think that these recommendations apply to you. After all, you might consume greasy pizza and sugared soda pop every day and feel just fine. Or perhaps you stay skinny no matter how many french fries and candy bars you eat.

There are plenty of reasons to swallow your pride

instead of a milkshake and pay attention to the guidelines, says Joan Lyon. She's a nutritionist at the United States Department of Agriculture (USDA) in Alexandria, Virginia.

Evidence continues to build that eating certain kinds of foods protects people from cancer, heart disease, obesity, diabetes, weak bones, and other health problems. Eating the wrong kinds of foods, on the other hand, causes your body harm.

As a dietician in the U.S. Army for 21 years, Lyon worked with a lot of young soldiers. They didn't think it mattered what they ate, she says. They felt like they were going to live forever.

But, if you don't pay attention to what you eat when you're young, Lyon says, it's really, really hard when you're old and you find yourself sick and unable to do much about it.

NEW INFORMATION

Every five years, the U.S. government enlists scientists to update a document called *Dietary Guidelines for Americans* and a food pyramid illustration that goes with it. As scientists learn more about the human body, nutrition, and disease, they adjust the guidelines to reflect the new information.

Lyon was a member of a large staff that helped a team

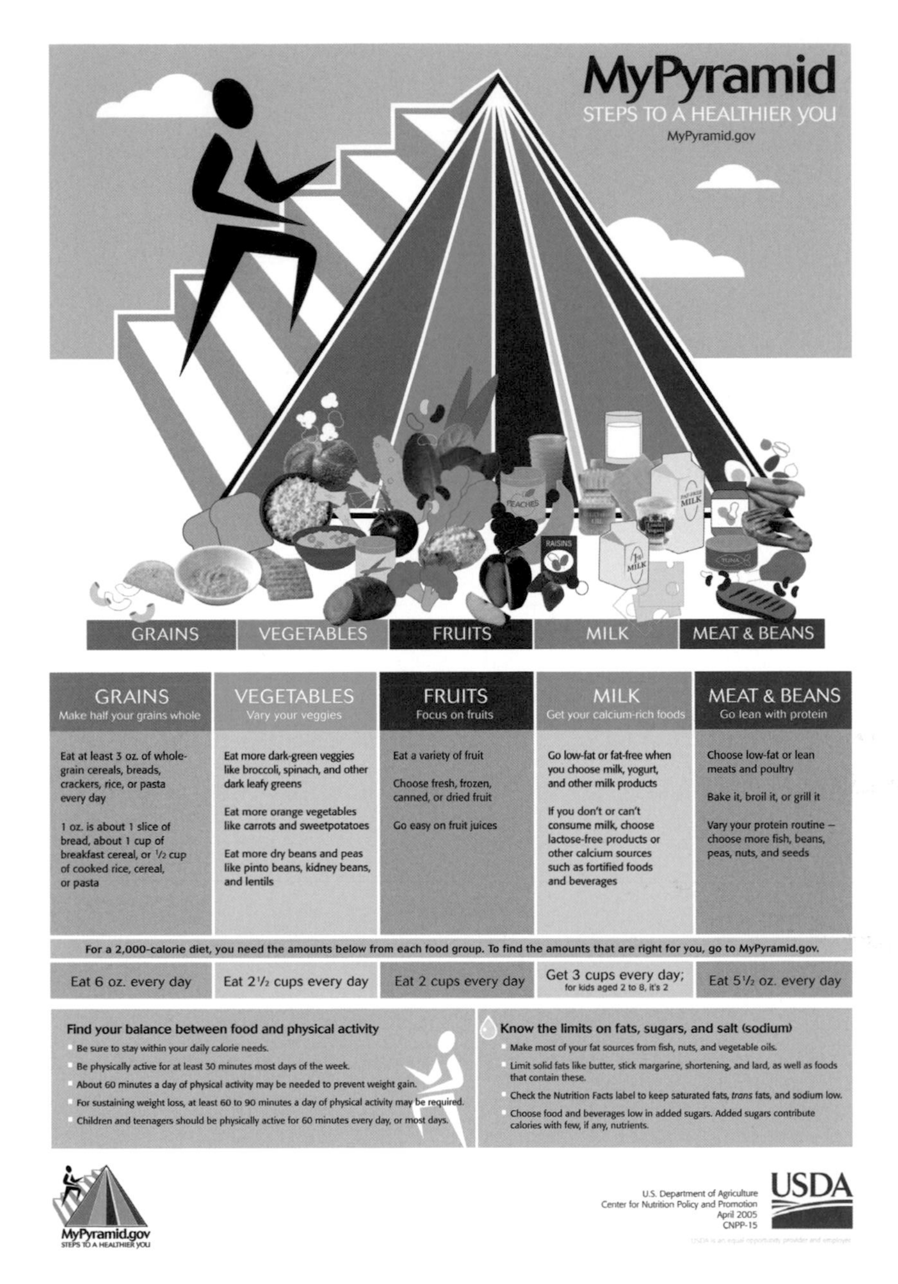

Figure 1.1 The new 2005 Pyramid differs from earlier guidelines in its emphasis on the importance of engaging in physical activity.

of 13 scientists put together the latest set of guidelines. The USDA and the Department of Health and Human Services released the guidelines in January 2005 (Figure 1.1).

Coming up with new guidelines every five years is a complicated process. More than a year before the new report is due, experts gather the latest scientific evidence on vitamins, minerals, and various foods. They discuss the findings. Sometimes, different studies seem to give opposite results. Sometimes, the evidence is incomplete.

"It's a very long process," Lyon says. "People can interpret science in different ways even when they're looking at the same data." It's sometimes tough to come up with firm conclusions that everyone agrees with.

- **Describe the process used to update *Dietary Guidelines for Americans*.**

And new discoveries keep coming along. A team of researchers in England and Denmark, for example, recently discovered a compound in carrots that appears to reduce a rat's chances of developing cancer.

This kind of study wouldn't have carried much weight with the USDA committee, though, because the scientists prefer to look at studies involving people. If researchers were to repeat the rat experiment with people and get similar results, the 2010 guidelines might end up suggesting that we eat more carrots.

WEIGHT CONTROL

More than the old guidelines, the 2005 recommendations focus on weight control, Lyon says.

"There's an energy equation," she says. "The calories you take in need to balance the amount of energy you expend in terms of physical activity and exercise, or you'll end up gaining weight. You need to make your calories work for you."

The best way to stay healthy, Lyon says, is to eat foods that are packed full of nutrients.

Instead of the five servings of fruits and vegetables that used to be recommended, the new guidelines suggest that adults eat even more than that: 2 cups of fruit and 2 1/2 cups of vegetables each day.

Kids should adjust the amounts of fruits and vegetables based on energy needs and size. It might be worth talking to your doctor or school nurse for advice on the amounts that are best for you.

The guidelines also recommend that people nine years old and up should drink three cups of low-fat or fat-free dairy products each day and eat lots of whole grains. Brown rice and whole-wheat bread, for example, are better choices than white rice and plain bagels.

Whole grains are important because they don't go through all of the processing that strips fiber, magnesium, calcium, and other nutrients from many starchy foods. Look on labels for ingredients such as whole oats and whole wheat.

The new recommendations distinguish between different kinds of fats, as well. Young people between the ages of 4 and 18 should get between 25 and 35% of their calories from fat, the experts say.

But most of this fat should come from nuts, vegetable oils, and fish. You should avoid a type called "**trans fats**," which appear on labels for cookies, crackers, and other foods as "hydrogenated" or "partially hydrogenated" oils.

As far as exercise goes, the document recommends 30 to 60 minutes of activity for adults on most days of the week and at least 60 minutes of exercise for kids every day.

- **In what ways do the 2005 food guidelines differ from those that were recommended in 2000?**
- **What information should you look for on a nutrition facts label on a food package?**
- **Why is exercise important? How much should kids get?**

CHANGING HABITS

As much sense as the new guidelines make, many people still have a hard time changing their habits, even when they know what's best for their health.

If you already eat lots of fruits, veggies, and whole grains, then keep up the good work. If you don't, Lyon says, try to start with just a few small changes, one at a time.

"Reach for fruit instead of candy," she says. "Try unsweetened beverages instead of soda. Get out and exercise and do physically active things with your friends." Eventually, these will become your new habits.

Long blamed for encouraging people to eat unhealthily, some companies are now joining in to help improve diets. Kraft Foods, for example, recently announced that it will stop advertising Oreos® and other snack foods to kids younger than 12. And General Mills recently began making all of its cereals with whole grains.

- **How are companies such as Kraft Foods and General Mills responding to unhealthy eating?**

More than ever, kids are making their own choices about how to spend their time and what to put in their mouths. Even if you feel fine, it might be worth learning how to read labels on the food you eat—and keeping the food guidelines in mind next time you order a meal.

"If you follow the guidelines," Lyon says, "they can help you feel better and look better. They can help you have clearer skin, healthier hair, and give you more energy."

Who could complain about that?

After Reading:

- Based on the food guidelines described in the article, do you think your school lunches are healthy? Why or why not?
- When you're establishing national guidelines for food, certain businesses can get upset. How do you think scientists and government officials would deal with, say, the makers of cookies or white bread?
- Suppose that one research team studying the health benefits of carrots might ask how many carrots certain people typically eat per week and link these numbers to how healthy these people are at a given moment. Another team might follow a group of people for 10 years or more, checking whether those who tended to eat more carrots per week ended up being healthier. Why would the results of these two studies on the same subject be difficult to compare? Why might the two studies give different results? Which study do you think would be more useful to scientists establishing new food guidelines? Why?
- Given all the benefits of eating healthily, why do you think more people don't eat that way?
- Come up with four ways in which you could become a healthier eater.

Body Mass Index and the Danger of Overweight

The United States today is by far the fattest society in the history of the world. Because fast foods and unhealthy snacks are so widely available and because high-tech conveniences like cars and vacuum cleaners mean we don't have to perform as much exercise to get our daily work done, more people are obese than ever before. The problem doesn't just affect adults; an alarming number of American kids are overweight. This is a serious issue, since childhood obesity can lay the groundwork for dangerous illnesses such as diabetes and heart disease.

To try to help people determine whether they are at a healthy weight, doctors have come up with a formula, called Body Mass Index, or BMI, which measures weight in relation to height. (See the Appendix for BMI charts.) As writer Emily Sohn shows in the following article, making sure your weight is within recommended limits and keeping track of how much fat you consume in your diet are two ways to live a healthy lifestyle.

—The Editor

ARTICLE

Packing Fat

by Emily Sohn

Before Reading:

- **What percentage of kids in the United States do you think are overweight or obese?**
- **Suggest some activities or habits that would help keep you from getting fat.**

The world is getting bigger—not the planet itself, but many of the people in it.

In developed parts of the world, from Australia to Europe to the United States, waistlines are bulging. People weigh more than ever before. Even children are joining the ranks of the obese in record numbers, and scientists are concerned.

"It's pretty obvious we have a problem here," says Ross Brownson. He's an **epidemiologist** at the St. Louis University School of Public Health in Missouri. "Most people would agree we have an **epidemic**," he says.

Stopping the obesity epidemic is one of Brownson's major goals. And he's not alone.

As part of the Institute of Medicine's Committee on Prevention of Obesity in Children and Youth, Brownson is one of 19 experts in the United States who recently released a report called "Preventing Childhood Obesity: Health in the Balance."

The report proposes ways to keep the nation's youth from getting fatter and fatter. The best solution, the experts say, is to get parents, schools, communities, governments, and kids themselves involved in tackling the problem together.

MORE THAN PUDGY

Many people can be a little pudgy around the tummy or the seat, but obesity is much more serious than that.

To see if someone is seriously overweight, doctors use a mathematical formula that takes a person's height and weight and spits out a number called the **Body Mass Index** (**BMI**). They then compare the person's BMI to those on a special chart (Figure 1.2).

In adults, a BMI between 18.5 and 25 is normal, greater than 25 is overweight, and greater than 30 is obese. An adult who is 5 feet, 5 inches [165.1 cm] tall, for instance, would have to weigh 150 pounds [68 kg] to be overweight and 180 pounds [82 kg] to be obese.

- **How do doctors figure out whether someone is obese?**

Childhood obesity is a little different. For one thing, age makes a difference. So does whether the child

Body Mass Index (BMI) Table

BMI	19	20	21	22	23	24	25	26	27	28	29	30	31	32	33	34	35
Height									*Weight (in pounds)*								
4'10" (58")	91	96	100	105	110	115	119	124	129	134	138	143	148	153	158	162	167
4'11" (59")	94	99	104	109	114	119	124	128	133	138	143	148	153	158	163	168	173
5' (60")	97	102	107	112	118	123	128	133	138	143	148	153	158	163	168	174	179
5'1" (61")	100	106	111	116	122	127	132	137	143	148	153	158	164	169	174	180	185
5'2" (62")	104	109	115	120	126	131	136	142	147	153	158	164	169	175	180	186	191
5'3" (63")	107	113	118	124	130	135	141	146	152	158	163	169	175	180	186	191	197
5'4" (64")	110	116	122	128	134	140	145	151	157	163	169	174	180	186	192	197	204
5'5" (65")	114	120	126	132	138	144	150	156	162	168	174	180	186	192	198	204	210
5'6" (66")	118	124	130	136	142	148	155	161	167	173	179	186	192	198	204	210	216
5'7" (67")	121	127	134	140	146	153	159	166	172	178	185	191	198	204	211	217	223
5'8" (68")	125	131	138	144	151	158	164	171	177	184	190	197	203	210	216	223	230
5'9" (69")	128	135	142	149	155	162	169	176	182	189	196	203	209	216	223	230	236
5'10" (70")	132	139	146	153	160	167	174	181	188	195	202	209	216	222	229	236	243
5'11" (71")	136	143	150	157	165	172	179	186	193	200	208	215	222	229	236	243	250
6' (72")	140	147	154	162	169	177	184	191	199	206	213	221	228	235	242	250	258
6'1" (73")	144	151	159	166	174	182	189	197	204	212	219	227	235	242	250	257	265
6'2' (74")	148	155	163	171	179	186	194	202	210	218	225	233	241	249	256	264	272
6'3' (75")	152	160	168	176	184	192	200	208	216	224	232	240	248	256	264	272	279

Source: Evidence Report of Clinical Guidelines on the Identification, Evaluation, and Treatment of Overweight and Obesity in Adults, 1998. NIH/National Heart, Lung, and Blood Institute (NHLBI)

Centers for Disease Control and Prevention
United States Department of Health and Human Services

Figure 1.2 Body Mass Index is a measurement of weight in relation to height. This chart shows BMI range for adults. Charts of BMI for boys and girls can be found in the Appendix.

is a boy or a girl. To be considered obese, a kid has to be in the top 5% of the BMI chart for his or her age.

According to the new report, some 9 million children in the United States over the age of 6 now qualify as obese. Over the last 10 years, obesity has become more than twice as common in children between the ages of 2 and 5 and in young people between the ages of 12 and 19. In the 6-to-11-year-old set, the rate has more than tripled.

HEALTH CONCERNS

It isn't just that being overweight might make it harder for you to drag yourself out of bed or off a couch. Obesity can cause serious health problems.

Studies show that weighing too much as an adult can lead to a variety of illnesses, including breast cancer, arthritis, and heart disease. Diabetes is a big one, too.

Diabetes makes it hard for the body to process sugar. It can develop in one of two ways. Some people are born with what's called "juvenile" (or type 1) diabetes, and their symptoms start in childhood. A second kind, often called "adult-onset" or type 2 diabetes, has traditionally tended to occur in obese adults.

- **Why has concern about obesity increased lately?**

With the spread of obesity to younger people, though, type 2 diabetes has followed.

"Over a 10-year period, studies show a 10-fold increase in the risk for diabetes in children," Brownson says. "We never used to see it in kids. Now, we're seeing . . . adult-onset diabetes in teenagers and even younger children."

Treating all these health problems is getting mighty expensive. Between 1997 and 1999, obesity-related hospital costs for kids averaged $127 million a year, up from $35 million a year between 1979 and 1981.

- **What illnesses have been linked to weight problems?**

If the obesity epidemic continues at its current pace, Brownson says, today's obese kids will cost the country an estimated $11 billion in the future.

There are other costs, too. People who are overweight often face a world that is unkind to them, and teasing can really take its toll. Depression and low self-esteem are common among obese people.

- **How has the cost of treating problems caused by obesity changed from 1979 to 1999?**

And the trend toward fat can be hard to break. Obese parents tend to have obese children. And obese kids tend to become obese adults.

DIET AND EXERCISE

So, how do you know if you're in danger of becoming obese?

Stepping on the scale won't necessarily give you an answer. Some people are naturally heavier than others, and that's okay.

Also, Brownson says, an overweight athlete is actually healthier than a thin couch potato. Muscle weighs more than fat and can skew the measurements.

To find out whether you should be concerned, it's best to talk to a doctor or school nurse, who can tell you more about how your weight fits in with the weight of others in your age group.

It can also help to learn more about the causes of obesity so that you can spot danger signs in yourself.

- **What could someone do if he or she were overweight and wanted to shed some pounds?**

People put on pounds when they take in far more **calories** than they use up. If you don't exercise enough and eat a lot of fatty or sugary foods, you could be in trouble.

Studies show that kids are watching more TV, playing more video games, and spending more time using the Internet than they used to. Many schools have cut their physical education programs. And few kids are walking or biking to school anymore. This means more time sitting and less time getting exercise.

"There's been a steady increase in how much time people spend in their cars," Brownson says.

At the same time, people are eating more and more. Portion sizes in restaurants have grown over the years, and most people can't help but eat more when there's more food in front of them.

Super-sizing is a bad choice when it comes to watching your weight. And sugary drinks may be part of the problem.

"Twenty years ago, we didn't have Big Gulps®," Brownson says. "The standard soda size was 8 or 10 ounces [0.24 or 0.3 l]. Today, it's 20 ounces [0.6 l]. That's a lot of calories to keep track of."

RESISTING THE URGE

Resisting the urge to indulge can be difficult, especially with the messages that pummel kids all day long. Everywhere you look, commercials, billboards, even scenes in movies try to persuade kids to buy junk food and sugary drinks.

The average child gets up to 40,000 hits of advertising and promotion every year, Brownson says. "If you've ever watched cartoons on Saturday morning," he says, you'd have seen that "they're not advertising a lot of fruits and vegetables."

To fight such pressure, Brownson says, kids can try to imagine what kinds of commercials they would design to spread the word about the dangers of obesity.

- **Name two ways in which TV plays a role in the obesity epidemic.**

The new report calls on local governments to make their cities and towns more “kid-friendly” with better bike paths, sidewalks, and playgrounds, and safer streets. It urges kids to spend less than two hours a day with computers and TVs so that they can spend more time running around. It asks schools to make physical activity a priority during the day. And it encourages families to eat well and do more activities together, including something as simple as after-dinner walks.

It helps kids a lot if parents set a good example. Parents influence what their kids eat. “You can’t have parents saying one thing and doing something else,” Brownson says.

Fighting obesity is a big job, but not a lost cause, Brownson says, as long as everyone works together.

“We have to be in this for the long haul,” he says. “We’ve taken decades to get into this mess. It’s going to take decades to get out.”

In the meantime, watch out for all those Halloween candies! They may be scarier than you think.

After Reading:

- Given that obesity is a serious problem, do you think it's more helpful to have action at the government level, programs in schools and neighborhoods, or efforts by individuals and families? Why?
- Why do you think more adults than kids are obese?
- Describe three lifestyle changes that you could make to become healthier.
- How do you think you're affected by TV ads for sugary snacks?
- Name three famous people who you think are healthy and three who are not. Explain the difference.
- Check the labels for the amount of sugar in a soda and five other food items that you eat or drink. Which of these foods has the most sugar per serving? Plot your findings on a chart.

Good Fats Versus Bad Fats

Although fat can be bad for you—it can cause obesity, diabetes, heart disease, and other chronic problems—there are certain types of fats in foods that actually make you healthier. These are called omega-3 fats, and are most commonly found in fish. In the following article, Emily Sohn explains the difference between "good" fats and "bad" fats, and shows how scientists are looking for ways to help us get more of the healthy fats we need into our diet.

—The Editor

ARTICLE

Moving Good Fats From Fish to Mice

by Emily Sohn

Fish is good for you. But if you can't stand eating fish, you might still be in luck. Thanks to some crafty genetic engineering, omelets, hamburgers, and other foods of the future could have some of the health benefits of fish, without smelling like the sea.

Fish such as trout and salmon are loaded with fats called omega-3 fatty acids. These fats are much better for you than the omega-6 fats found in red meat or poultry. Omega-3 fats make your heart healthier. Omega-6 fats do the opposite.

Amazingly, worms known as **nematodes** have a gene that converts omega-6 fats into omega-3 fats. A group of researchers from the Massachusetts General Hospital in Boston wanted to see if they could tap into the power of this particular gene. So, they took it out of some worms and put it into some mice. The experimental mice were then raised on the same diet as a group of normal mice.

After 8 weeks, muscle tissue from the experimental mice had more omega-3 fat than omega-6 fat. This was a huge improvement. Normal mice have far more omega-6 fat than omega-3 fat.

Researchers hope eventually to be able to put this worm gene into cows and chickens. The resulting milk, beef, and eggs would then be rich in good fats and as healthy for your heart as a slab of grilled salmon.

Don't be surprised if worm genes someday wind up enriching your milk or yogurt. Your taste buds won't notice the difference, but your heart will reap the rewards.

Going Deeper:

Harder, Ben. "Gene Transfer Puts Good Fats in Mammals." *Science News* 165 (March 6, 2004): 157. Available online at *http://www.sciencenews.org/articles/20040306/note12.asp*.

You can learn more about healthy and unhealthy fats in foods online at *www.kidseatgreat.com/efacids.html*.

Section 2

Food and Your Body

Everyone knows that eating a healthy, balanced diet helps keep the body in good shape. What you may not realize, though, is that certain kinds of foods affect different parts of the body. Eating these foods can help protect your brain, your bones, or your muscles. If you don't get enough of these essential nutrients, you risk some very specific health problems. The articles in this section examine some of the latest findings about the role of various foods in maintaining the health of different body parts or systems.

The first article looks at antioxidants—special chemicals that protect the cells of the brain from damage caused by aging, environmental hazards, and the action of free radicals. Free radicals are chemicals that can break down and destroy body cells, causing irreversible damage. A diet rich in antioxidants can help stop free radicals and keep your body going strong.

This section also explores recent scientific studies about how so-called "comfort foods"—like ice cream or your favorite dinner—can actually have a chemical effect on the brain to reduce stress and make us feel better. It's possible that we crave certain foods because our bodies need the nutrients they contain to help decrease our stress levels.

Finally, this section discusses the importance of nutrition for bone health. You probably already know that not getting enough calcium in your diet can lead to osteoporosis, a dangerous condition in which the bones deteriorate. Through the recommendations of food scientists, you can take action now to build strong bones and avoid health problems far into the future.

—The Editor

Antioxidants in Your Diet

Everyone knows that fruits and vegetables are good for you, but what you may not know is that different colored foods may have special health benefits. Brightly colored fruits and vegetables, from blueberries to broccoli, are loaded with a special kind of chemical called antioxidants. Antioxidants help protect the body's cells from damage caused by pollution, the ultraviolet light of the sun, and even skin wrinkles. In the following article, *Science News for Kids* writer Sarah Webb examines antioxidants and the foods in which they are found, explaining how a diet based on a wide variety of colorful fruits and vegetables can help you live a long, healthy life.

—The Editor

ARTICLE

The Color of Health

by Sarah Webb

Before Reading:

- **Name five brightly colored fruits or vegetables.**
- **Describe what you would consider a healthy meal.**

Plants and animals often use color to attract attention. Deep, rich colors also provide another, important benefit for plants. Scientists have shown that the substances responsible for these colors actually help protect plants from chemical damage.

"When we see plants, we see a lot of different colors," says Wayne Askew. "In particular, we see a lot of reds and greens and yellows." Askew is a professor of nutrition at the University of Utah.

The good news for us is that, when we eat colorful fruits and vegetables, the **pigments** (or colorings) protect us, too.

BUILT-IN SUNSCREEN

The pigments responsible for plant color belong to a

class of chemicals known as **antioxidants**. Plants make antioxidants to protect themselves from the sun's ultraviolet (UV) light.

Ultraviolet light causes chemicals called **free radicals** to form within plant cells. If free radicals move through plant cells without being neutralized or eliminated, they can begin to destroy parts of the plant. Antioxidants stop free radicals in their tracks, shielding cells from harm.

Typically, an intensely colored plant has more of

Antioxidants

Plants can produce a variety of antioxidants. Not all of them are pigments (and not all pigments are antioxidants).

Here are some examples of potent antioxidants that can be found in various fruits and vegetables:

- Vitamin C (ascorbic acid) — oranges, tangerines, sweet peppers, strawberries, potatoes, broccoli, kiwi fruit
- Vitamin E — seeds, nuts, peanut butter, wheat germ, avocado
- Beta carotene (a form of vitamin A) — carrots, sweet potatoes, broccoli, red peppers, apricots, cantaloupe, mangoes, pumpkin, spinach
- Anthocyanin — eggplant, grapes, berries
- Lycopene — tomatoes, pink grapefruit, watermelon
- Lutein — broccoli, brussels sprouts, spinach, kale, corn

these protective chemicals than a paler one does.

- **What role do antioxidants in plants play?**
- **How are free radicals in plants created?**

Free radicals aren't a problem just for plants. They also affect people and animals. And ultraviolet light isn't the only source of these damaging chemicals.

If you breathe polluted air, such as smog, automobile exhaust, or discharges from a factory, you take in chemicals that also cause such damage, Askew says. And, the body itself produces free radicals as it processes food.

WHITE SUIT

All organisms use oxygen to convert food into energy, just as burning wood in a fireplace produces heat. At the same time, oxygen is involved in the production of free radicals that are often very similar to compounds needed by a cell to stay healthy.

Free radicals are like a friendly dog that's just been out in the mud, says James Joseph. He's a nutrition researcher at Tufts University. If you play with the dog while wearing a white suit, the dog will leave muddy paw prints. Unfortunately, the dirt may permanently stain the suit.

It's not as if the dog meant to hurt you, Joseph says. After all, it didn't try to bite you. It merely wanted to bond with you.

Figure 2.1 This artist's depiction shows how free radicals—seen at top left as blue spheres with purple centers—attack the cells of the body.

Similarly, free radicals can bond with **molecules** in a cell, changing the molecules into forms that aren't as useful or good for the cell as the originals were (Figure 2.1).

For example, free radicals can attack **lipids**—molecules that form a fence around cells to allow only certain chemicals to travel in and out of cells. They can also damage **DNA**, the genetic material that serves as the master plan for a cell and governs how it works. Proteins, the molecules in a cell that actually do the work of processing food, also face problems if they run into free radicals.

In general, free radicals can keep a cell from functioning properly.

- **What are lipids?**

SUNSCREEN ON THE INSIDE

Our bodies have natural defenses for fighting off free radicals. The body makes certain molecules, known as antioxidants or repair enzymes, that stop free radicals before they can harm us. It's like a video game of opposing chemical reactions in which good-guy repair enzymes battle bad-guy free radicals for control of cell and body.

While we're young, our defenses are pretty strong. However, our natural defenses get weaker as we get older. The body's built-in stoppers can only go so far without extra help.

And we can sometimes see the effects of free-radical, or oxidative, damage directly. Wrinkled skin, for example, is one sign of skin-cell damage. Certain cancers and heart disease are linked to free radicals. Overeating and obesity are linked to **oxidative** damage.

- **How is wrinkled skin related to free radicals?**

We can help by sending in reinforcements: antioxidants. For people, this means a lifestyle of consistently eating a variety of fruits and vegetables with intense colors. Joseph compares eating fruits and vegetables to "putting on sunscreen for the inside of your body."

In early 2005, the U.S. Department of Agriculture [USDA] released new guidelines that recommended we eat five to nine servings of fruits and vegetables each day.

COLORFUL FOOD

The key to fighting free radicals with fruits and vegetables is to mix and match colors. Go for very bright colors and for many different colors (Figure 2.2).

If you're looking for greens, spinach, broccoli, and dark green lettuces do the job. Pale iceberg lettuce packs little chemical bang per bite. For reds, strawberries and other berries are best, and tomatoes are tremendous. Carrots, oranges, sweet potatoes, and squash all shine among the yellow/orange foods.

In general, fresh fruits and vegetables are great, but dried or frozen forms of these foods can also be healthy.

Blue or purple foods, in particular, can be very beneficial, Joseph says. Have blueberries, Concord grapes, and eggplant, for example, on your menu as often as you can. These blue foods contain hundreds of healthful chemicals not found anywhere else, he says.

NEWS DETECTIVE by Sarah Webb

Have you ever stopped and really looked at the produce section of a grocery store? Until recently, I'd just walk through, buy one or two items, and move on. I'd never appreciated the beauty of a store's collection of fruits and vegetables.

The colors amaze me. Sunny oranges, deep green spinach leaves, lusciously red strawberries, and dark, shiny eggplants show the range of colors in nature's palette. And, like an explorer looking at a new and distant place, I've become more adventurous with color in the kitchen these days.

I've spent years working in a chemistry lab, and I like to mix ingredients and see what happens. The nice thing about cooking is that I can experiment safely when I prepare a meal. If I add too much of an ingredient, my food might not taste very good, but at least it won't explode.

Lately, I've taken the time to make a pasta sauce with tomatoes, green peppers, mushrooms, onions, garlic, and various spices. Making it taste good is my own little chemistry experiment.

I'm eating more spinach. I get a lot of my green that way—mostly in salads. I also snack on dried fruit. Apricots and cranberries are my favorites, and I'm happy to know that they have lots of antioxidants. I already love blueberries.

What's great is that nature has worked out such a wonderful way to protect both plants and the animals that eat plants. With color as a clue, it's not hard to figure out which plants are going to have the most free-radical-busting punch per bite.

It's comforting for me to know that, while I'm enjoying myself in the kitchen, I'm promoting good chemistry on the inside, too.

Joseph's research on how chemicals in blueberries affect brain function in rats even suggests that these chemicals may help our own brains work more efficiently. Wouldn't it be nice to be both healthier and smarter?

AN ANTIOXIDANT VITAMIN?

Antioxidants are just chemical compounds. Why can't we just make a good antioxidant pill?

Figure 2.2 To protect your body against free radicals, food scientists recommend that you eat a diet full of brightly colored fruits and vegetables, which are loaded with free-radical-fighting antioxidants.

People who have tried to make pills with antioxidants in them have found that the pills don't seem to work as well as eating the fruits and vegetables themselves.

The different amounts of different antioxidants in the same food appear to work together to fight free radicals more effectively than the ingredients do by themselves, Askew says.

Nature has already worked out the right balance in plants. Scientists have a long way to go before they'll really understand how much of each antioxidant chemical works best.

- **When you are selecting fruits and vegetables for maximum health benefit, what should you look for?**
- **What makes blueberries especially healthy? See *http://oregonblueberry.com/health.php* (*Oregon Blueberry Commission*).**

So, the next time you're at a supermarket, you can shop for your own personal chemistry experiment. Pick out interesting fruits and vegetables with lots of different colors, then get to work in the kitchen. You might try preparing something that you've never tasted before, or you just might create a meal that's both beautiful to look at and delicious to eat.

And, as you digest your meal, those colorful antioxidants will start doing their own chemistry on the inside, neutralizing free radicals and keeping you healthy.

After Reading:

- Come up with a menu for the most colorful, antioxidant-rich meal that you can imagine.
- Green tea is often mentioned as a food high in antioxidants. Why do you think this is the case? See *www.umm.edu/altmed/ConsHerbs/GreenTeach.html* (*University of Maryland Medical Center*).
- Summarize in your own words the relationship between antioxidants and free radicals.
- Go to the grocery store and look at packaged fruits and vegetables. Which packages list antioxidants?
- Imagine that you work at the U.S. Department of Agriculture. Write a brief report listing why it's important to eat five to nine fruits and vegetables a day. Find at least two books or articles to support your ideas.
- If you wanted to grow antioxidant-rich fruits and vegetables in your backyard or even on your windowsill, what sorts of plants could you use in your area?

Comfort Foods and Your Health

We all have favorite foods—which tend to be unhealthy items like ice cream or candy—that we associate with good times and fun, such as birthdays or celebrations. These kinds of foods are often called "comfort foods," since we feel better emotionally when we eat them. As writer Emily Sohn explains in this article, scientists have found out how the chemicals in our favorite foods interact with our body chemistry to cause these good feelings, which makes us want to enjoy these foods again and again, even if they may not be the right choices for a healthy lifestyle.

—The Editor

ARTICLE

Turning to Sweets, Fats to Calm the Brain

by Emily Sohn

When you get really nervous about a soccer tournament or a school play, do you ever get the urge to eat a whole box of chocolates or a bowl of ice cream? If so, you're not alone.

In times of stress, many people turn to french fries, ice cream, macaroni and cheese, and other fatty "comfort foods" to make themselves feel better. There might be important biological reasons for those cravings, according to a new theory.

Studies with animals and people have shown that stressful situations cause the body to churn out lots of extra **hormones**, including those known as **glucocorticoids**. These chemicals eventually shut down the stress response, and the animal relaxes.

If the stress lingers for days and days, however, glucocorticoids no longer shut down the stress response. Animals may then begin to seek out yummy foods. All of those extra calories get stored as fat around the waist. Then, in a feedback loop, this abdominal fat interferes with the action of the glucocorticoids, and the animal relaxes again. In this way, studies with rats show, comfort foods really can ease anxiety.

That's the theory at least.

In our society, however, enduring stress is such an established fact of life and comfort foods are so easy to get that stressed-out people often gain weight. That increases their risk of heart disease, diabetes, and other health problems.

Pay attention to your cravings. If you catch yourself mindlessly reaching for the cookie jar, stop and take a few deep breaths. It may be time to take a vacation instead!

Going Deeper:

Ramsayer, Kate. "Sweet Relief: Comfort Food Calms, With Weighty Effect." *Science News* 164 (September 13, 2003): 165–166. Available online at *http://www.sciencenews.org/20030913/fob5.asp*.

You can learn more about stress online at *http://www.bam.gov/head_strong/top10Coping.htm* and *http://www.bam.gov/survival/physical_signs.htm*.

Using Food to Prevent Bone Loss

We all know we should eat a variety of foods that are rich in vitamins and minerals to stay healthy, but many people, especially young people, are often most concerned about gaining weight and don't recognize other dangers that can result from an unbalanced diet. One of the most pressing health problems in our society is osteoporosis—the breakdown of bones caused by a lack of calcium in the diet. Women are particularly vulnerable to this condition, which can make bones weaken and break easily. As Emily Sohn points out in the following article, the time to start taking steps to prevent osteoporosis is while you are young. By making sure you include plenty of bone-building foods in your diet and getting plenty of exercise, you can make your bones strong and healthy for life.

—The Editor

ARTICLE

Strong Bones for Life

by Emily Sohn

Before Reading:

- **What do you think could happen if you don't take care of your bones?**
- **What sort of nutrition is important for kids to make sure they develop strong bones?**

If you're like most kids, you probably think you'll never get old. Achy joints, failing eyesight, heart attacks: These are things you won't have to deal with for a long time, right? So why worry now?

As it turns out, the choices you make now can make a big difference in how you feel later in life. I recently learned this lesson the hard way.

It started with an injury: a cracked shinbone caused by too much running on hard pavement. My doctor suggested a bone scan, which showed that my bones are weaker than average. I don't have osteoporosis, a disease that causes older people to shrink in height and break bones easily. But I'm close.

For me, the diagnosis was a scary wakeup call. I'm just

27 years old, but already I'm worried about things that normally happen only to women more than twice my age. Will I break my hip if I slip on a patch of ice? Is it safe for me to go skiing, lift heavy boxes, play Ultimate Frisbee®?

Perhaps what upsets me most is the realization that I might have avoided all of this if only I had thought ahead earlier in life. Childhood and adolescence are the most important times to build strong bones. For you, there's still time. Doctors suggest a variety of foods you can eat and exercises you can do as a teenager to build strong bones for life.

LIVING TISSUE

Bones are amazing. They're hard but flexible, and they're lightweight but tough. Without bones, we'd be just puddles of skin and guts.

An adult person has 206 bones in his or her body (Figure 2.3). The outer layer of a typical bone is made of a hard material honeycombed with tunnels. This web of hollow pipes allows a bone to be strong and light. It also allows the passage of nutrients and waste. A protein called **collagen** gives a bone its elasticity. Chemicals known as calcium salts make a bone hard.

But, even though our bones support us, they're easy to ignore. Unlike a cut or bruise, a weak bone isn't visible or painful.

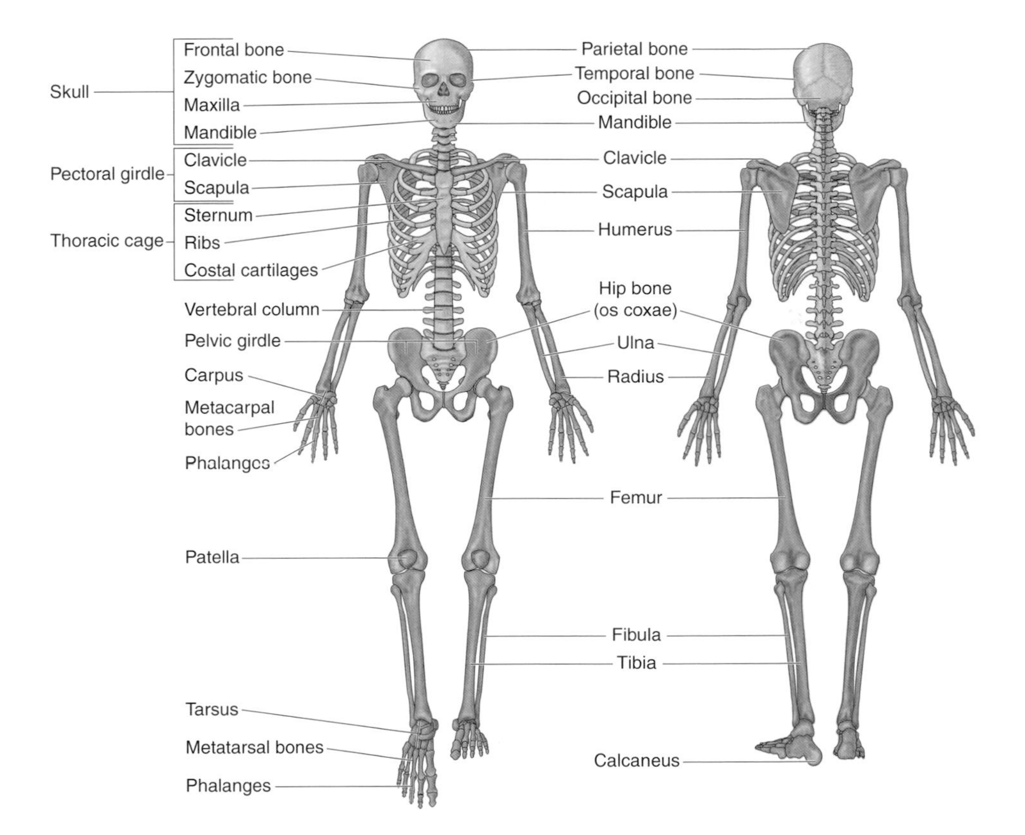

Figure 2.3 Adults have 206 bones in their body, and all of them need good nutrition—especially in the form of calcium—to stay strong.

Osteoporosis is sometimes called a silent disease. People often don't realize they have it until it has progressed so far that they break bones while doing ordinary things, such as walking down stairs or lifting heavy objects.

Osteoporosis happens mostly to older people. But I'm not the only woman in her 20s with weak bones. Increasingly, scientists are finding that weak bones are a problem in teenagers and even younger kids. That's especially troubling because youth is the critical time for bone growth.

If you've ever seen a skeleton in a museum, you might think that bones are dead. In fact, bones are living tissue. They reshape and rebuild themselves many times as you grow and age.

- **What is osteoporosis? How can you tell if you suffer from osteoporosis?**

The cycle of building and breaking down bone changes over a person's lifetime. Bone-building is fastest during the first three years of life and again during adolescence. By the time you're in your 20s, the tissue in your bones is about as tightly packed as it's going to get.

Measuring something called bone density tells you how tightly packed the bone tissue is. A high bone density normally shows that you have strong bones.

Once you get to be about 35 years old, bone tissue gets broken down more quickly than it's replaced. This

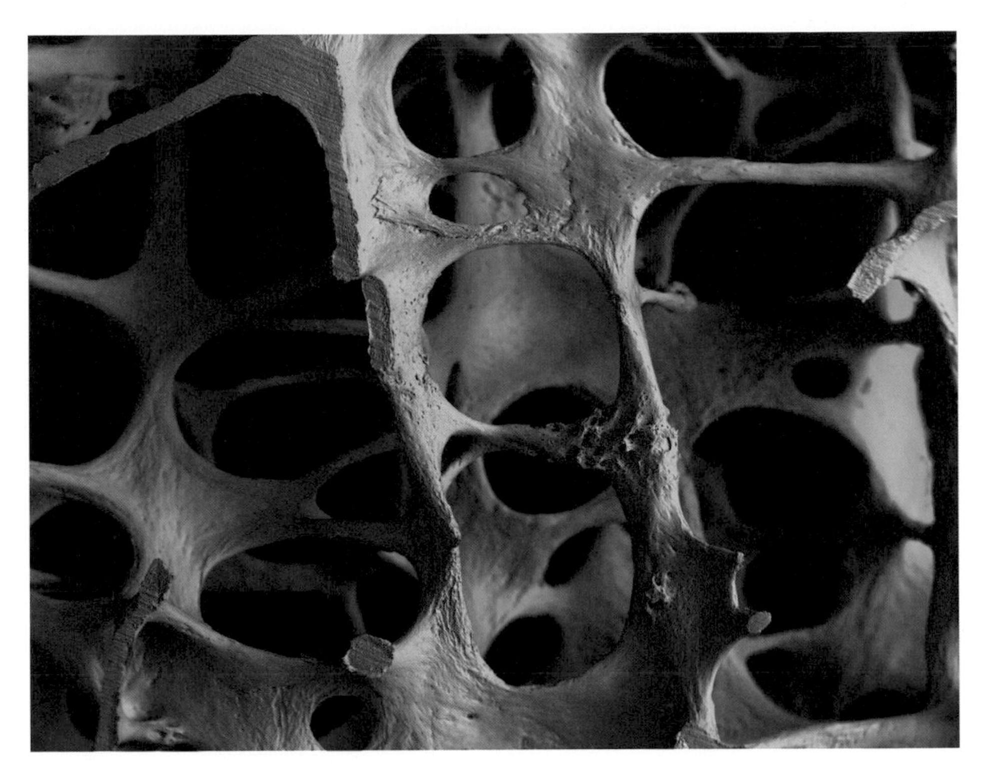

Figure 2.4 Osteoporosis makes bones much more porous—and, therefore, weaker—than they should be, as seen in this magnified photo of the bone of a woman with osteoporosis.

means that bones tend to lose tissue, and the bone density goes down (Figure 2.4). That's when osteoporosis usually becomes a concern. And it's a bigger risk for women than for men.

FOOD CONCERNS

Getting the right kind of bone-building nutrition and exercise as a teenager is like putting money in the bank. Your bones can stay strong as you get older.

Unfortunately, many teenagers don't think about their bones when they order lunch or decide what to do with their free time. They'd rather snack on chips or slurp soda than think about vitamins.

And parents don't always set the best example. "I was standing by the elevator at Children's Hospital," says Susan Coupey, an adolescent medical specialist at Children's Hospital at Montefiore in Bronx, New York. "There was a two-year-old child being fed soda by his parents."

Junk food has few nutrients. It also fills you up, so you don't eat enough of the good stuff. That's one reason why many adults want schools to get rid of soda machines.

Doctors urge kids to get plenty of calcium, the mineral that makes bones strong. Calcium is also essential for keeping nerves, blood, and muscles healthy. When you don't take in enough calcium, your body takes calcium out of your bones, which weakens your bones even more.

- **What role does calcium play in bones?**

Although calcium is abundant in milk, yogurt, cheese, fortified juices, soy milk, and some nuts and vegetables, few people get enough of it. The Institute of Medicine recommends that kids between the ages of 9 and 18 get 1,300 milligrams of calcium every day. That's roughly the amount of calcium in a quart of milk.

Yet fewer than 10 percent of girls and 25 percent of

boys get that much, according to the National Osteoporosis Foundation. "The average calcium intake of adolescent girls in the United States is somewhere around 900 milligrams," Coupey says. "Many take in just 600 to 700 milligrams."

PAYING ATTENTION

Now that I've started paying attention, I realize that getting enough calcium takes some effort. Getting 1,300 milligrams of calcium is equivalent to drinking about 4 glasses of milk, eating 10 cups of cooked broccoli, or having 2 glasses of milk, a cup of yogurt, and a glass of orange juice—every day!

And that's not all you need. To absorb the calcium you eat, you have to take in a variety of other vitamins and minerals, including lots of vitamin D.

- **Why is it better to consume milk or yogurt than a soft drink?**

In the summertime, you get vitamin D from sunlight on your skin. Where I live in Minnesota, though, it's too dark and cold much of the year to spend a great deal of time outside. To get the recommended 400 to 800 international units of vitamin D recommended for people my age, I drink 2 cups of fortified milk every day, and I take a vitamin supplement. The American Academy of Pediatrics now recommends that teenagers take a daily multivitamin that has 200 international units of vitamin D.

Getting enough exercise is also crucial. "There have been some really excellent studies showing the effectiveness of weight-bearing exercise and strengthening exercises on bone density," Coupey says.

Any exercise at all is better than sitting in front of the TV. Walking and lifting weights, in particular, are great for building muscles that support and strengthen bone. Playing soccer, tennis, or basketball are also good options.

A recent study found that elementary school girls who did jumping exercises for 10 to 12 minutes, 3 times a week, built 5 percent more bone mass than did girls who didn't do the exercises. That's enough bone mass to buy women some extra bone strength later in life, said the scientists from the University of British Columbia who did the study.

- **Besides changing your diet to include more calcium, what else can you do to strengthen your bones?**

Even if you're glued to the TV set, why not do some jumping jacks during the commercials? Have a glass of milk or fortified juice and some almonds instead of a can of soda and chips.

The changes are small, but the payoff could be big. You might even be amazed at how good it feels to take care of your bones. Support them, and they will support you for many years to come.

After Reading:

- **Given the suggestions provided in this article for protecting and increasing the health of your bones, do you think you're doing a better or worse job than most of your classmates? Why?**
- **Do you think there should be soda machines in schools? Why or why not?**
- **What suggestions would you offer to a friend who wants to protect her bones but is allergic to milk products?**
- **How do bones change over time?**
- **Create a three-day menu of meals (breakfast, lunch, and dinner) that would help prevent bone weakness.**
- **Coupey suggests that people do "weight-bearing exercise and strengthening exercises." Name three sports in which players would get such exercise.**

Section 3

Eating What You Like

Just about every day, we're bombarded with information on television, radio, and the Internet about how important it is to use food to stay healthy. With all these media messages, it can be easy to forget that food has traditionally been something to enjoy, a way to have fun with the people we love. Sometimes, we may become so worried about whether we're eating the "right" things that food just doesn't seem like fun. It is essential to remember that, as long as you use moderation, you can still have the foods you love.

This section takes a look at some of the most popular "comfort foods" of all time: french fries, cheese, and, of course, chocolate. Although food scientists devote a lot of their time to researching the health properties of various foods, that is not all they do. Many food scientists work with companies and restaurants to help find ways to produce better-tasting, easier-to-cook varieties of the foods we love.

In the first article, we examine chocolate, which is almost everyone's favorite snack. Author Emily Sohn delves into the history of chocolate, showing how the seeds of the cacao tree are turned into the tasty treat we love, and exploring the efforts of food scientists to make chocolate even better.

The second article looks at cheese, a food that has been made and enjoyed for almost as long as human beings have been on this planet. We learn about how food scientists are studying ways to make cheese melt more evenly, to improve foods like pizza and mozzarella sticks.

Finally, we examine french fries. Although most of us love our fries crispy, oily, and salty, we know they're not good for us. This article explores how food scientists are hard at work trying to find a way to make our favorite side dish better for us, so we can enjoy it more often.

—The Editor

Our Love Affair With Chocolate

It's hard to find someone who *doesn't* love chocolate. It's one of those foods that has had a deep influence on our lives. We use it to celebrate holidays, to reward ourselves after a tough job, and we share it with the people we love. Chocolate doesn't just taste good. Scientists have determined that chocolate causes our brains to release chemicals that improve our mood and make us *feel* better. Some experts even argue that certain types of chocolate may be healthy for us—in moderate amounts, of course. In this article, writer Emily Sohn looks at our love affair with chocolate, describing how it is made, how it affects our bodies, and new advances in food science that may make the chocolate we enjoy even better.

—The Editor

ARTICLE

Chocolate Rules

by Emily Sohn

Before Reading:

- **Where does chocolate come from?**
- **What qualities are important in a good chocolate bar?**

For a lot of people, there's no better taste combo than chocolate and nuts. For food scientists, though, this combination is a major headache.

Nuts contain oil, says Greg Ziegler, who studies chocolate at Pennsylvania State University. The nut oil tends to seep, or diffuse, into the chocolate. This process softens the chocolate, which also turns a chalky color. People no longer want to eat it.

Oil diffusion is just one of many problems that chocolate scientists face in creating the different kinds of chocolate sold in stores. Depending on the type of cocoa beans, processing conditions, and ingredient proportions, chocolate products can end up with differ-

- **Why is the combination of nuts and chocolate a problem for food scientists?**

ent flavors, textures, shapes, sizes, and even nutritional properties.

Chocolate products of all sorts are in great demand, especially around holidays and for special occasions. In December, for example, you can buy dark chocolate

I swoon after a bite of really fancy chocolate, but I don't care much for the cheap stuff. I don't eat large amounts of it, and I don't crave it every day. In other words, I'm a chocolate lover, but a picky one.

So, I was delighted when I learned about the "Twin Cities Chocolate Extravaganza," a chocolate show held in Minneapolis in November 2004. It sounded like the perfect setup. Some 35 companies, mostly local, would set up exhibit booths to introduce people to their chocolate products. Tickets cost $10 in advance. Samples were unlimited. It was bound to be an amazing day.

It turned out even better than I expected. Samples included cherry-filled truffles, deluxe chocolate ice cream, chocolate-chip cheesecake, and a spicy, rich chocolate drink, based on a classic Mexican recipe. There were also lectures and demonstrations, but I was too busy eating to attend any of those.

Nevertheless, I learned a lot of things. One vendor, for instance, showed me what cocoa beans look like before and after they're roasted. I also learned that if you succes-

Santas and crispy chocolate reindeer. Around Easter, there are hollow chocolate bunnies and cream-filled chocolate eggs. For Valentine's Day, stores are filled with lots of chocolate candies.

As appetizing as these treats may be, it's the science

sively sample pieces of chocolate made with different proportions of cocoa powder, you can really tell the difference. The more cocoa powder there is, the richer and more intense the chocolate tastes.

Eating a lot of chocolate also leads to a mighty buzz. After just 10 or 15 minutes of standing in lines and sampling truffles, my hands were shaking. My heart was racing. I was talking quickly, and I couldn't stop smiling.

"I am having such an amazing time!" I said to my friend Ariane. She laughed. She knew exactly how I felt.

My final lesson came as a mighty shock. There is such a thing, I discovered, as eating too much chocolate. After the show, I felt sluggish and slightly queasy. I was crashing.

Later, at home, I made myself an enormous salad, full of every green and healthy item I could find in the fridge. When I went to bed, I figured I wouldn't need another piece of chocolate for a long time.

Funny enough, the next morning I woke up craving hot cocoa and chocolate-chip muffins. A little bit does go a long way. But there always seems to be room for more!

behind chocolate that helps determine which types people choose to eat. And, despite years of research, exactly which combinations of factors make some types tastier or more appealing than others remain a mystery.

It's a mystery that chocolate companies are eager to solve—and one that keeps chocolate scientists busy.

"The process of making chocolate is very complex," Ziegler says. Despite a lot of work, "there are no hard and fast answers yet."

WORK IN PROGRESS

Chocolate, as we know it today, has been a work in progress for thousands of years.

People in Mexico and Central America were the first to pluck seed-containing pods from cacao trees and grind the seeds (or beans) into a powder for a spicy, frothy, bitter drink.

The explorers Christopher Columbus and Hernando Cortés brought cocoa beans back to Europe early in the 1500s. Even then, no one knew quite what to do with the beans because the resulting drink tasted so bitter. Finally, Cortés had a brilliant idea: Add sugar!

Sweet drinking chocolate rapidly became a special treat for royalty across Europe. As production increased, chocolate grew cheaper and more popular. Finally, in the 1800s, advances in England and Switzerland led to the creation of solid chocolate, which people still crave today.

MAKING CHOCOLATE

The basic process for making chocolate hasn't changed much since the 1800s. After beans are removed from their pods, they go through a few days of fermentation to get rid of some of the bitterness. Then, the beans are dried, either in the sun or under hot-air pipes.

- **How is chocolate made? See *www.exploratorium.edu/exploring/exploring_chocolate/choc_5.html*.**

Finally, the beans are shipped to candy companies, where they are cleaned, sorted, and roasted for anywhere from 30 minutes to 2 hours. Both roasting time and temperature (250°F [121°C] or higher) have a big effect on how the chocolate tastes in the end. So do drying methods, bean variety, and growing conditions, including temperature, moisture, and soil composition.

Once roasting is finished, the beans are crushed and separated into three parts: a bitter liquid called chocolate liquor; a fatty, yellow solid called cocoa butter; and a powder that is often used in cakes and cookies (Figure 3.1).

Dark chocolate has just three main ingredients: chocolate liquor, cocoa butter, and sugar. The liquor, which is not alcoholic, is the bitter part. Sugar counters

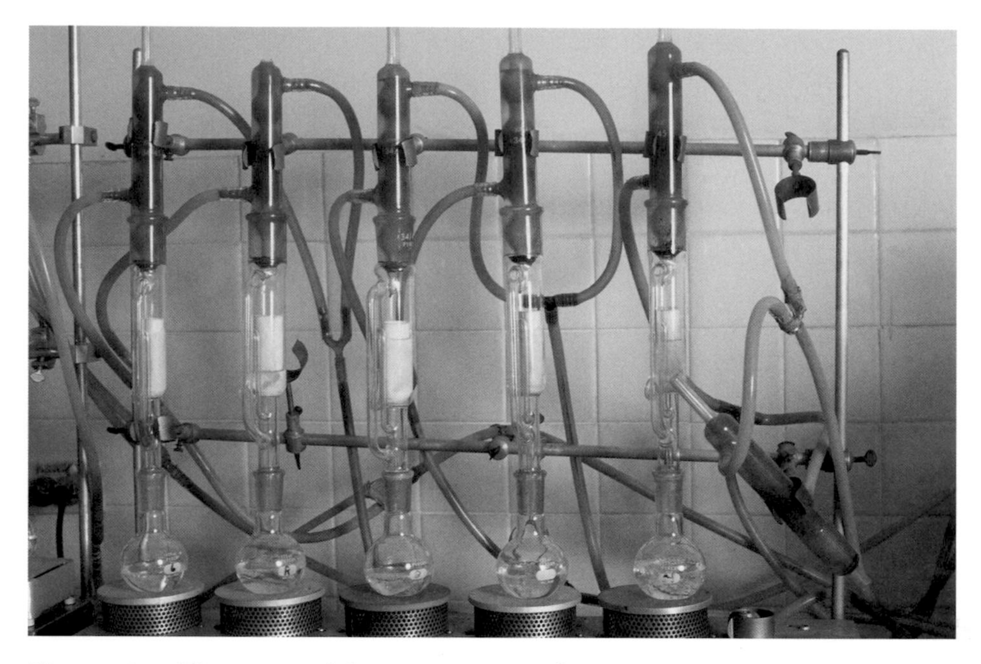

Figure 3.1 These machines separate the components of chocolate from cocoa beans into chocolate liquor, cocoa butter, and powder.

the bitterness, and the cocoa butter adds fat. Milk chocolate also contains milk solids. White chocolate is just sugar, milk solids, and cocoa butter, with no liquor.

Less than 1% of a finished chocolate product is made up of flavorings, such as vanilla and salt. There's also often a small amount of an **emulsifier**, such as soy lecithin, which keeps the sugar suspended and spread out in the solid. If you check the ingredients label on the back of a chocolate bar, you might see soy lecithin in the list.

- **What's the difference between milk, white, and dark chocolate?**

FLAVOR EXPERIMENTS

Playing with the ratios of the main ingredients and adding fillings are two major ways in which manufacturers experiment with flavors. One look at the candy aisle shows how far chocolate research has come. Modern chocolate bars include everything from almonds and raisins to caramel and cookies. Some bars are crispy; some are chewy; some are frozen.

With each new flavor or texture combination, however, comes a new puzzle. Edges are one major challenge, Ziegler says. Coatings tend to thin out at the corners of a bar.

Then, there's the nut problem. After years of research, scientists have come up with strategies for making nutty chocolate last longer. Some companies, for example, create bars that place a physical barrier, such as a candy coating, between the chocolate and the nuts or peanut butter.

Being selective about the type of cocoa butter is another way to slow diffusion. Varieties of cocoa butter that are extra-solid work best. It also turns out that there are six different kinds of crystals that can form inside cocoa butter. Some of these forms are more resistant to oil diffusion than others.

- **What's one strategy that manufacturers can use to keep nut oil from getting into chocolate?**

Still, plenty of questions remain. Ziegler is pretty sure that nut oil actually dissolves in cocoa butter. This process, he suggests, is what ruins the chocolate's texture and color. Other scientists propose that chocolate acts more like a sponge, sucking up the oil through a process called capillary infiltration.

"Right now," Ziegler says, "the most important thing is just to get a handle on what physical phenomena are involved." He and his colleagues have used special equipment to get detailed images of what goes on over time inside a piece of nut-filled chocolate.

Eventually, he hopes to come up with a mathematical equation that predicts how nuts and chocolate behave (or misbehave) together. This information could then be used to create products that last longer.

"We might find out that it's not only different crystal types but also the size of crystals in the fat that are important in determining how quickly the oil dissolves," he says. "Then, we could change the crystal proportions."

GOOD TASTE

While Ziegler is hard at work on the nut quandary, other researchers are trying to breed cocoa beans that are resistant to disease but still taste good. Their biggest challenge is to figure out why some beans have hints of flowers, fruits, or raisins, among other flavor notes, and why some beans produce superb chocolate and others don't.

Still others are busy experimenting with textures and sensations. That melt-in-your-mouth quality may in fact be what you crave more than the way the food itself tastes.

In one study, scientists showed that swallowing chocolate-filled capsules didn't satisfy cravings for chocolate nearly as much as actually chewing pieces of chocolate. The researchers concluded that the special sense of well-being that comes from eating chocolate has more to do with the experience itself than with anything actually in the chocolate.

- **Describe three ways in which scientists are trying to improve the taste or texture of chocolate.**

Yet, even though its chemical makeup may not fuel your cravings, the way chocolate affects your body has become a major focus of chocolate research in recent years. Scientists have discovered that chocolate contains compounds called **flavonoids**, which might protect against heart attacks, keep you from getting sick, even help cure coughs. Yes, it's true. Eating chocolate can actually be good for you!

- **What are flavonoids, and what do they do? For additional information about flavonoids, see *www.cacaoweb.net/nutrition.html*.**

So, eat up. Just make sure to keep your portions reasonable. Despite the wonders of chocolate, it's still loaded with sugar and fat, and no one should eat too much of those.

"It tastes good, and it makes you happy," Ziegler says. "In moderation, it's okay."

Better yet, consider becoming a chocolate scientist. "It's a dream job," Ziegler says. "I like science and figuring things out and understanding nature. But for me, my specific work on chocolate seems to open a lot of doors. It makes people happy. When I tell them what I'm working on, they smile."

Spread the joy. Don't just eat chocolate. Study it!

After Reading:

- Why do you think many people enjoy the taste of nuts and chocolate together?
- What types of scientists are needed in the chocolate industry?
- Do different nuts affect chocolate differently? Design an experiment to answer this question.
- Some people don't like chocolate; others love it. Why do you think people react differently to chocolate and other foods?
- What other foods besides chocolate can give you a "melt-in-your-mouth" sensation?
- Check the list of ingredients on the wrapper of your favorite chocolate bar. Find out as much as you can about each of the ingredients, including what it's for. You can learn more about food labels and ingredients at *http://anrcatalog.ucdavis.edu/pdf/8108.pdf* and *http://www.mrkland.com/fun/xocoatl/bars.htm*.

Cheesy Research

People have been producing different kinds of cheeses for thousands of years. Making cheese is a complex process that turns liquid milk into a solid treat. From macaroni and cheese to mozzarella sticks, cheese forms the basis for many of our favorite foods, and there's a kind of cheese for every taste.

Cheese may taste delicious, but most cooks will tell you that it isn't always easy to work with. It can melt unevenly, and can turn too lumpy or too stringy. To try to solve this problem, food scientists have been looking at new ways of producing cheese, to make it easier to use and even tastier to eat.

—The Editor

ARTICLE

A Taste for Cheese

by Emily Sohn

Before Reading:

- **Why do you think cheese is a popular food?**
- **If you were a food scientist, how would you try to improve cheese?**

Chances are you love cheese. You might put cheddar on your crackers, Swiss on your sandwiches, or melted Colby on your hamburgers. You probably go gaga over a bowl of gooey macaroni and cheese and nuts over cheesy nachos. You eat pizza any chance you get.

"There really is no good excuse not to like cheese," says Lloyd Metzger. He's a dairy food chemist at the University of Minnesota, Twin Cities.

With thousands of varieties available and more in the works, there's a cheese to fit nearly any taste preference, Metzger says. "If you like stinky cheese, you can find a cheese to fit that flavor profile," he says. "If you like bland cheese, you can find that, too."

Metzger has developed an especially fine appreciation for cheese. As a scientist who studies this multipur-

NEWS DETECTIVE by Emily Sohn

An hour before I visited the cheese lab at the University of Minnesota in St. Paul, the milk truck broke down. It was supposed to deliver 3,000 pounds [1,361 kg] of fresh milk. Without it, Lloyd Metzger and his colleagues had to scrap their plans to make havarti and dill havarti cheese that day.

I wasn't completely out of luck, though. Cheese maker Jodi Ohlsen Read had leased space in the lab to work on her recipe for a cheese called Sheep's Milk Bleu. Read owns a farm called Shepherd's Way, near Northfield, Minnesota, about an hour south of St. Paul. She makes most of her cheese on the farm, but when she needs to work out some kinks in a new recipe, she likes to use research equipment at the university.

When I arrived at the lab, Read and her assistant, Josh Dix, were tending to a huge vat full of a thick, yogurt-like substance. The milk had already been heated, **pasteurized**, and mixed with salts, enzymes, and molds. Now they were cutting it by hand into mini-marshmallow-sized chunks. As they sliced with a large metal knife, the curds solidified, releasing lots of watery **whey**.

At one point, Read handed her cutting tool to Ray Miller, coordinator of the university's cheese plant. She calls him a "cheese **guru**" because he has lots of experience. And he can rattle off cheese statistics with impressive speed and accuracy. Miller also happens to be very tall.

"He makes it look effortless," Read said, as she watched Miller slice through the cheese like butter. "That's not the case."

Making cheese is hard work. I worked up a sweat just watching the process.

Nevertheless, cheese scientists are a dedicated bunch. After 12 years as a writer, Read switched to making cheese, and she has never looked back.

"The best part is the magic of it," Read said. "You start with milk at the beginning of the day, and you end up with all of these little cheeses. You are creating something."

Miller the guru, whose father was in the cheese business for more than 40 years, has been eating and working with cheese for most of his life. His favorite part about making cheese is the scientific aspect.

"It's a fascinating science," he says. "Cheese is a living system. Even when it's in the cooler ripening, chemical reactions are taking place. Enzymes are breaking things down, increasing flavor compounds. It's always changing. No two lots of milk are identical. It's a variable system, but you know you have to create consistency."

Science aside, there's also a much simpler pleasure in being a cheese scientist, Metzger says. "It's nice," he says, "to be able to eat your work."

pose food, he makes and tastes cheese in his laboratory two or three times a week.

Along with other researchers around the world, Metzger is working to formulate cheeses that are tastier, more nutritious, or easier to make than those now in stores.

More than just your taste buds stand to benefit from cheese research. Cheese making is a big business, too.

Every year, each person in the United States eats an average of 33 pounds [15 kg] of cheese, according to data published by the Food and Agriculture Organization of the United Nations. Denmark, Greece, and France top the list, with 63, 57, and 54 pounds [29, 26, and 25 kg] per person, respectively.

That's a lot of cheese.

- **Who eats more cheese per person per year: people in the United States, France, Greece, or Denmark?**

MAKING CHEESE

Loving cheese is nothing new. People have been making it for at least 5,000 years, maybe longer. The first cheese-makers, most experts agree, were herders in the Middle East who domesticated goats and sheep and figured out how to milk them.

Legend has it that someone once stored milk in a saddlebag made from the stomach of an animal. After a while, lumps developed in the milk, thanks to a stomach enzyme in the bag called **rennet**. *Voilá*! The first cheese was born.

Turning liquid milk into a solid food had advantages. Compared to milk, cheese was easy to transport, and it could be stored for a longer time. It also tasted good.

- **What's one popular story about how cheese was first made?**

The basic process of making cheese hasn't changed much since those first lumps accidentally formed thousands of years ago. Scale is probably the biggest difference.

Instead of using animal stomachs to process milk from a few homegrown cows, Metzger says, large cheese companies now use room-sized vats that hold 50,000 gallons [189,271 l] of milk.

Once in the vat, milk is often heated to kill harmful **bacteria**. Manufacturers then add rennet, which is extracted from animal stomachs. Proteins in milk normally float around as separate molecules. Rennet makes them stick together.

Within 30 or 40 minutes, the enzyme turns the milk's proteins into gel-like yogurt clumps called curds. Stirring utensils and knives in a machine cut the curds into small pieces (Figure 3.2). As the mixture becomes more concentrated over the next 3 to 5 hours, a liquid called whey seeps out.

- **Where is the enzyme rennet found?**

Figure 3.2 Cheese making is a complicated and highly scientific process that requires a lot of training and skill.

Companies use whey to make high-protein shakes and other products. For every 100 pounds [45 kg] of milk, 90 pounds [41 kg] of whey escape, leaving just 10 pounds [4.5 kg] of cheese to chew on. First, though, there's still more work to do.

Bacterial cultures and salts go in next. The types that are added determine what kind of cheese you end up with. The variety of milk (including what kind of animal it comes from and what the animal was eating before it was milked) also makes a difference, as do storage conditions.

Swiss cheese, for instance, goes through a unique ripening process with a certain type of bacterial culture that generates gas, putting holes in the cheese. Cheddar cheese goes straight into the refrigerator. As the cheddar sits there, however, proteins break down, creating a "sharper" flavor. The longer it sits, the sharper the cheese gets. Sometimes, aging goes on for years.

- **What makes Swiss cheese different from other cheeses?**

PERFECT MELT

To dig deeper into the science of cheese, Metzger works with a special cheese-making machine. One of his main goals is to develop a mozzarella cheese that melts and stretches the way pizza makers would like it to. It's a search for the "perfect melt."

"One problem right away when you make mozzarella," Metzger says, "is that it doesn't have the texture that you want."

When it's freshly made, mozzarella cheese releases a lot of water when it's heated, and it doesn't melt into that stretchy, smooth blanket of chewy goodness sought out by pizza lovers far and wide. Only after about 30 days in the refrigerator does fresh mozzarella develop the properties you see in pizza ads.

If you've ever had fried cheese sticks that were watery, the problem might have been a batch of cheese that was too fresh. "The cheese sticks out of the breading, and it leaks all over," Metzger says. "We want to prevent the cheese from having a lot of flow, but we still want it to have a big, long stretch."

It's the composition of the protein network in mozzarella that determines how stringy the product ends up, Metzger says. And proteins normally take time to break down.

So, Metzger and his colleagues are experimenting with different kinds of bacterial cultures that might help chop up these proteins more efficiently. They're also working with concentrations of calcium, because the mineral acts like cement to hold the structure of cheese together.

"What we're trying to do," Metzger says, "is to

change how we make mozzarella so it performs the way we want it to right away."

PROCESSED CHEESE

- **Why do pizza chefs need to let mozzarella sit?**

Metzger also works with processed cheeses. Kraft Foods started making these products in the 1920s, and they have grown more and more popular ever since. They were first developed as a food that could be safely shipped to soldiers overseas without spoiling.

Foods such as Velveeta® are made out of fresh cheese, but they're heated and mixed with salts that turn the cheese into what's called an **emulsion**. The result is a squeezable, free-flowing food that can last indefinitely.

The popularity of processed cheeses has created a growing demand for consistency. People want their cheese products to taste the same every time.

With so many factors involved, including milk that changes in flavor every season, creating tastes on demand can be a big challenge for cheese manufacturers. To meet these demands, Metzger and his colleagues use high-tech microscopes and other equipment to analyze how cheese proteins and fats interact in different concentrations.

The final product also depends on how much mixing occurs or what type of emulsion salts are added. During processing, "things are always changing," Metzger says. "It's a constant battle to keep things in spec."

- **How is processed cheese different from traditional cheese?**

WORK OF ART

At places such as the Northeast Dairy Foods Research Center at Cornell University in Ithaca, New York, and the California Dairy Foods Research Center in Davis, scientists are developing new ways to make low-fat cheese, new types of packaging to preserve cheese longer, cheeses that freeze well, better techniques for making cheese quickly and cheaply, and more.

Yet, as scientific as the process has become, cheese making in many places remains a work of art, designed to please the eye as well as the palate. On modest farms from France to Wisconsin, people tinker with small batches of fresh organic milk to make beautiful blocks of flavorful cheese that are different every time. Despite the costs, demand is high.

- **In what ways are dairy researchers trying to improve cheeses and the process of cheese making?**

"For $20 a pound, you can have art and something special," Metzger says. Or you can gnaw on a hefty chunk of cheddar for a fraction of that price. Thanks to science, there's something for everyone.

After Reading:

- Making cheese can involve a lot of science. What other foods do you think might require a similar level of scientific and engineering expertise and research? Why?
- What kind of science would a person interested in studying cheese need to know?
- What problems might come up if you were trying to lower the fat content of a cheese? For information about developing a low-fat cheese, see *www.chancellor.wisc.edu/yourworld/2223.html*.
- Design an experiment that involves cheese.
- What advantages might cheese makers who use small batches of milk have over large-scale producers?
- People often eat cheese-flavored snacks, such as Doritos®, Cheetos®, or Cheez-It® crackers. How do manufacturers add the cheese flavor to such foods? For information on flavoring snack foods, see *www.foodproductdesign.com/archive/1997/0597AP.html*.
- Many people can't drink milk or eat dairy products. Why does this happen? See *www.sickkids.on.ca/kidshealth/spring02vol3issue1/gotmilk.asp*.

Can French Fries Be Good for You?

With the popularity of fast-food restaurants, Americans today are eating more french fries than ever. Although fries come in many varieties—from thick-cut steak fries to the thin, crispy, highly salted kind served as McDonald's—they are rarely considered a health food. Because almost all fries are cooked in fatty oils, they have long had a bad reputation among doctors and food experts. Knowing how popular french fries are, scientists are working hard to find ways to make this old favorite healthier, as writer Emily Sohn explains in the following article.

—The Editor

ARTICLE

In Search of the Perfect French Fry

by Emily Sohn

Before Reading:

- **How would you describe the perfect french fry?**
- **How do you think french fries are made?**
- **Do you like fried foods?**

I'm among the minority: My favorite french fries are thick, homemade, and full of steamy potato flavor with the skins left on.

Fighting over the meaning of french-fry perfection may seem like a silly thing to do. But the stakes are huge: People spend more than $75 billion on fried foods every year (Figure 3.3).

Yet those same foods have a terrible reputation among nutritionists. The more fried foods Americans eat, the fatter they get, and the more likely they are to develop diabetes, heart disease, and other health problems.

Two teenagers in New York even tried to sue McDonald's in 2002 for making them fat. The case was dis-

- **How much money do people spend on french fries each year?**

Figure 3.3 French fries come in many different shapes and sizes to suit every taste, but they are not known for having high nutritional value.

missed, but the problem remains: Is it possible to make a yummy french fry that's also good for you?

BUILDING BETTER FRIES

Now, after years of careful observation and experimentation, research is showing that maybe we can have our fries and eat them, too.

Using basic principles of chemistry and engineering, scientists are finding new ways to make better fries that strike a balance among flavor, texture, and nutrition. Their work may eventually propel french fries into a more modern version of perfection.

Next time you're in a fast food restaurant, watch carefully as the fry cook plunges a batch of uncooked potato strips into the fryer.

On a typical day at McDonald's, oil temperature in the fryer averages a steamy 340°F [171°C]. The potatoes—which are usually partially pre-fried and then frozen—are much colder than that. So when the cook throws them in, water inside the potatoes starts to boil immediately, and bubbles rise to the surface.

As water evaporates from the potatoes, holes open up for oil to creep in, and a crust forms from the outside in. The crust soon approaches the temperature of the oil, while the soft interior of the potato continues to hover at about 212°F [100°C], the boiling point of water.

During the three minutes or so of deep frying, you can watch the bubbles rise slowly at first, then a little faster, then slower again in an enormous cycle that scientists call "**heat transfer**." Without it, a potato will always be just a potato.

"We feel very strongly that this dynamic, variable heat transfer is one of the primary things that makes frying unique and leads to those products we love," says Brian Farkas, a food engineer at North Carolina State University.

- **What is the process used by McDonald's to make french fries?**

OIL AS THE CULPRIT

Oil has traditionally been the secret behind making a fantastic fry. Oil tastes good, and it gives fries the kind of texture, or "mouth feel," we find so pleasing.

But from a health standpoint, oil is the enemy—loaded with calories, fats, and cholesterol. As much as 20% of a french fry's calories come from oil.

So for years, scientists have been trying to mimic the heat transfer of the frying process without using oil. Results have been only so-so.

One major focus of oil-free research has involved blasting a partially fried potato with fast-moving air as hot as 400°F or 500°F [204° or 260°C], using a hair-dryer-like machine. The Ore-Ida Company even developed a french-fry vending machine based on the technique.

"They weren't too bad," Farkas says hesitantly, but they weren't too good, either. "The problem is that when you blow hot air across the fries, you blow the oil off, and you make a mess. You don't get the kind of heat transfer unique to frying."

Some scientists have tried using chemically engineered, low-fat oils such as olestra to make healthier fries. But those oils have come under fire for being impossible to digest, and they're expensive to make.

Other researchers have been working to makc cdiblc coatings that keep oil from penetrating the potatoes.

Another idea on the table is to pack potatoes full of vitamins, through engineering or other processes, says Michael Blumenthal, an ex-oil chemist who is now a food consultant.

- **List one advantage and one disadvantage of the following methods:**
  - **Frying in oil**
  - **Using fast-moving air**
  - **Using low-fat oil.**

FORTIFIED FRIES

Surveys have shown that one-third of vegetables eaten by preteens and one-quarter eaten by teenagers in the United States are potatoes, Blumenthal says, most of which are fried.

"That's unbelievable," he says. "There are not many nutrients in french fries. So if that's the way society is going, then just like bread, french fries should be fortified."

Perhaps the most promising new technique for making fries that are good and good for you involves infrared energy—the kind emitted by a heat lamp.

By zapping potatoes with infrared energy at high enough intensities, Farkas says he can turn a **tuber** into a pile of ash in minutes. But by controlling the level of intensity to mimic the heat transfer involved in frying, it might be possible to produce more perfect fries.

"In the end," he says, "they will hopefully have lower oil content and all the desirable qualities of french fries."

NEWS DETECTIVE by Emily Sohn

I first found the french-fry scientists when I was in graduate school in Santa Cruz, California, in 2000. My assignment was to write a feature story about something science-related. It would be my first long story, and I wanted to find a topic that involved lots of science but that would be interesting to everyone, even people who think they don't like science.

After an extensive and increasingly frantic search as my deadline approached, I came across a Website for the food science department at the University of California in Davis. Research topics ranged from "the role of dietary fat in tissue function" to "interactions of **microorganisms** in foods." Boring, boring. Then, I came across Professor Paul Singh's home page and descriptions of his research into fried foods. Bingo!

For me, the topic was especially dear. "French fry" was actually my first word. As a very young child, I pronounced it "fry fry" by mistake, but I loved the crispy, salt-drenched things, and I still do. Pretty soon, my feature found a focus: the scientific search for fried-potato perfection.

To report the story, I made the two-hour drive from Santa Cruz to Davis one weekend in March. It just so happened I had a terrible flu and fever at the time, but I still managed to visit Singh's lab to meet with him and his colleagues. Even as I constantly blew my nose and coughed up my lungs, the researchers showed me their equipment, which included industrial fryers, thermometers, and a sophisticated poking machine called the Texture Analyzer, which looks like an overgrown 3-D Hangman board, and measures the crispiness of fried potato patties. Here's an excerpt from the original story:

The experiments require three people to make sure every patty gets measured the same way. Because texture changes with temperature and time after frying, the scientists run from fryer to Texture Analyzer, with stopwatches, thermometers, and cutting knives in hand. They wear special gloves and safety glasses to avoid the splatter of hot frying oil. They measure crust resilience, and they conduct "stress relaxation tests," which rate potato patties for their ability to bounce back after compression. They test each crust 15 times.

I also spent a few hours at a local McDonald's restaurant, just watching batches of fries go into the fryer again and again. I timed how long the fries stayed in the oil, and I took notes on temperature and other details. I got a lot of funny looks and comments from customers. Many of them wanted to know if I was an official french fry inspector!

To really round out my research, I thought it was important to do some of my own sampling. So, for a few weeks while I was working on the story, I ate as many french fries as I could. I tried them at every restaurant around town, and I asked waiters and waitresses lots of questions about what kind of potatoes they used and how they were cooked. Funny enough, I never got sick of them. In fact, for me, knowing where french fries come from makes the eating experience even richer!

TASTE TEST

In a McDonald's restaurant in California a while back, one stringy-haired, 10-year-old girl didn't hesitate for a second to give me her opinion about perfection in the french fry world.

"McDonald's are the best because they're salty and good," she said. Sometimes kids know things in a way that scientists can't match.

After Reading:

- **Having read the article, what would make the ideal french fry for American society?**
- **What don't you know about how McDonald's makes their french fries?**
- **Who would you agree with in the McDonald's lawsuit, the teenagers or McDonald's?**
- **Do you think it is possible to make a yummy french fry that is good for you? Why or why not?**
- **After reading this article, has your opinion about fried foods changed? How?**

Appendix

Body mass index-for-age percentiles: Boys, 2 to 20 years

BMI

34
32
30
28
26
24
22
20
18
16
14
12

kg/m²

97th
95th
90th
85th
75th
50th
25th
10th
5th
3rd

2 3 4 5 6 7 8 9 10 11 12 13 14 15 16 17 18 19 20

Age (years)

Published May 30, 2000.

SOURCE: Developed by the National Center for Health Statistics in collaboration with the National Center for Chronic Disease Prevention and Health Promotion (2000).

CDC

SAFER • HEALTHIER • PEOPLE™

Published May 30, 2000.
SOURCE: Developed by the National Center for Health Statistics in collaboration with the National Center for Chronic Disease Prevention and Health Promotion (2000).

antioxidants: Substances that prevent chemical reactions caused by oxygen or free radicals.

bacteria: Single-celled microscopic organisms that may cause disease.

Body Mass Index (BMI): Measure of the ratio of the weight of the body in kilograms to the square of the person's height in meters.

calories: One calorie is the amount of heat needed to raise the temperature of water by 1°C [33.8°F]; calories are used to measure the amount of energy in foods.

collagen: Fibrous protein found in vertebrate animals that makes up connective tissues and bones.

diabetes: Disorder in which the pancreas does not produce insulin properly, so that the body has problems processing glucose.

DNA: Deoxyribonucleic acid; substance that serves as the molecular basis for heredity.

emulsifier: Substance that causes emulsion, a mixture of two unblendable substances.

emulsion: A mixture of two substances that cannot be blended.

epidemic: An outbreak of disease.

epidemiologist: A scientist who studies diseases and disease outbreaks.

flavonoids: Oxygen-containing antioxidant compounds that contain many pigments.

free radicals: Reactive atoms or groups of atoms that have one or more unpaired electrons.

glucocorticoids: Corticosteroids that play a role in the metabolism of carbohydrate, protein, and fat.

guru: A teacher and intellectual guide.

heat transfer: The movement of heat from an object of higher temperature to one of lower temperature.

hormones: Substances that circulate in the bloodstream and help control the activities of cells.

lipids: Substances that are among the main components of living cells; lipids include fats and waxes.

microorganisms: Living things that are too small to be seen without the aid of a microscope.

molecules: Substance made up of one or more atoms that still retains all the properties of the individual atoms.

nematodes: Long cylinder-shaped worms that may live as parasites on the bodies of animals or plants or freely in the soil or water.

osteoporosis: Condition in which bone mass decreases, causing bones to become porous and fragile.

oxidative: Refers to chemical reactions that involve oxygen.

pasteurized: Refers to a method of treating liquids, such as milk, by exposing them to a particular temperature for a period of time to destroy disease-causing organisms without substantially changing the properties of the liquids themselves.

pigments: Substances that produce color.

protein: Substance made up of amino acid residues joined together with peptide bonds.

rennet: The lining membrane of the stomach of an animal, used to curdle milk.

tempeh: An Asian food made by fermenting soybeans.

tofu: A soft food made by treating soybean milk to make it coagulate.

trans fat: A fat that contains unsaturated fatty acids.

tuber: A short fleshy plant that usually grows underground.

whey: The watery part of milk that is separated from the curdled part when making cheese.

Books

Gardner, Robert. *Health Science Projects About Nutrition*. Berkeley Heights, NJ: Enslow Publishers, 2002.

Gold, Susan Dudley. *The Skeletomuscular System and the Skin*. Berkeley Heights, NJ: Enslow Publishers, 2003.

Landau, Elaine. *A Healthy Diet*. New York: Franklin Watts/Scholastic, 2003.

Smolin, Lori A., and Mary B. Grosvenor. *Basic Nutrition*. Philadelphia: Chelsea House Publishers, 2004.

Websites

Dietary Guidelines for Americans 2005
http://www.healthierus.gov/dietaryguidelines/

History of Chocolate (Field Museum)
http://www.fieldmuseum.org/Chocolate/history.html

Institute of Medicine: Prevention of Childhood Obesity
http://www.iom.edu/report.asp?id=22596

KidsHealth
http://kidshealth.org

United States Department of Agriculture: Food Pyramid
http://mypyramid.gov/

U.S. Food and Drug Administration
http://www.cfsan.fda.gov/

Trademarks

Big Gulp is a registered trademark of 7-Eleven Inc.; Cheetos is a registered trademark of Frito-Lay, Inc.; Cheez-Its is a registered trademark of Keebler Company; Doritos is a registered trademark of Frito-Lay, Inc.; Frisbee is a registered trademark of Wham-O Inc.; Oreo is a registered trademark of Nabisco, Inc.; Velveeta is a registered trademark of Kraft Foods Inc.

Picture Credits

page:

3: © Corel Corporation
16: U.S. Department of Agriculture
25: Centers for Disease Control and Prevention,
U.S. Department of Health and Human Services
37: © Corel Corporation
42: Mediscan/CORBIS
46: © Corel Corporation
55: © Lambda Science Artwork
57: © Alan Boyde/Visuals Unlimited
65: © Corel Corporation
72: Owen Franken/CORBIS
84: Craig Lovell/CORBIS
92: Klaus Stemmler/zefa/CORBIS
100–101: Centers for Disease Control and Prevention,
U.S. Department of Health and Human Services

Contributors

EMILY SOHN is a freelance journalist, based in Minneapolis. She covers mostly science and health for national magazines, including *U.S. News & World Report*, *Health*, *Smithsonian*, and *Science News*. Emily divides her time between writing for kids and writing for adults, and assignments have sent her to countries around the world, including Cuba, Peru, and Sweden. When she's not working, Emily spends most of her time rock climbing, camping, swimming, exploring, and pursuing adventures outdoors.

TARA KOELLHOFFER earned her degree in political science and history from Rutgers University. Today, she is a freelance writer and editor with ten years of experience working on nonfiction books for young adults, covering topics that range from social studies and biography to health and science. She has edited hundreds of books and teaching materials, including a history of Italy published by Greenhaven Press. She lives in Pennsylvania with her husband, Gary, and their dog and cat.